Just Passing Through

poems by

M. Scott Douglass

Paycock Press
Arlington, Virginia

Cover art and book design: M. Scott Douglass
Produced in the United States of America by
Main Street Rag Publishing, Charlotte, NC
www.MainStreetRag.com

Acknowledgments:

Asheville Poetry Review: "The Body of Her Work"
Final Friday Reading Event Anthology: "Poetry Reading at a Biker Bar (as "Jessica"),"On the Road to Weymouth"
Gargoyle: "Finding Iowa," "Math Don't Lie," "Sunset Over Suburbia," "You Know These Roads"
Iodine Poetry Journal: "Relentless," "At Bruegger's This Morning," "On the Road to Weymouth"
Midwest Review: "She Won't Drive with You Through Kansas or Nebraska"
North American Review: "When You Think of Hannibal, MO"
Plainsongs: "Pacing Yourself"
Poetrybay.com: "Kentucky Rising"
San Pedro River Review: "Where Are You"
Slipstream: "First Impressions," "Roadside Fantasies"
Tar River Review: "Second Skin"

Library of Congress Control Number: 2017913303

ISBN-10: 0-931181-57-7
ISBN-13: 978-0-931181-57-3

Paycock Press
3819 North 13th Street
Arlington, VA 22201
www.gargoylemagazine.com

for Jill

Contents

I. Journey

II. Travelers

III. The Road Itself

I. JOURNEY

Reflections On The Road

Waiting for breakfast at
a Cracker Barrel near Elkin
in *Andy of Mayberry* land

you watch one elderly woman
lead another on her arm through
the dining area. The second woman

is smaller, more fragile, old enough
to be the first one's mother,
with an ageless look of wonder

in her eyes, a child-like expression
as if witnessing her first lit
Christmas tree on Christmas Day.

Or maybe you're imagining. Maybe
morning light from open blinds
is reflecting off her glasses.

But you've seen this look before, heard
the soft shuffle of feet unlearning
the security of ground, heard

muffled voices of fellow travelers
who no longer recognize street signs,
no longer know what road they're on.

And you wonder what it's like
to be lost within yourself. Is every day
a taxi ride around the same block

or do you wake each morning
like a tourist in a foreign land
eager to rush out into the street,

grasp the hand of a stranger, bask
in the warmth of each new experience,
a never-ending epiphany?

She Won't Drive with You
Through Kansas or Nebraska

These are only two of many
    places she'd rather fly over.

She says, "When you've seen
    one pasture, you've seen them all."

You counter with a debate of corn
    versus wheat versus soy,

of drought versus drowning,
    healthy versus sick,

of sunflowers waving
    in fading light, the golden glow

of morning dew in late summer,
    air kissed with a hint of must.

You remind her of a blue rowboat
    beached amid Nebraska grasslands

of fleeing funnel clouds springing
    up and down over distant prairie,

the fluorescent green innuendo
    of terraced Iowa fields in spring.

This treasury of accidents
    you witnessed together, lost

or smeared on muddy canvas
    from thirty thousand feet.

Why You Hate to Fly

A boy with earbuds works an iPhone
with two thumbs as he ambles through
the airport, bumps into a trash can
and drops the device in front
of a middle-aged woman in leopard-
skin leggings, sleeveless T, and stilettos
as she stomps toward a distant gate.
She stops abruptly, reroutes, struts on.

Mom is carrying sister. Dad
is herding carry-ons. Young Game Boy
is engrossed in a world of violence
without consequence.

A woman on the people mover turns
and talks to the man behind her, hands
flailing with expressive compulsion.
You wonder if she talks in her sleep,
if her partner ever sleeps or wakes
with multiple contusions.

Mom tells Game Boy to hurry,
keep up. He can't hear her, doesn't
want to be here or wherever they
are going, and you can relate.

You wish every lady wearing
leopard-skin tights or flaunting a voice
loud enough to drown out jet engines;
every passenger with unchecked bags
or newborn; every woman who thinks
the concourse is a fashion show runway;
wish they all would stay home, wish
the girl at check-in would hand you keys
like they do at the Hertz counter,
offer you safe travels, a nice flight,
and send you on your way.

What Makes You Stronger

Shot and a beer, shot and a beer.
shot,
    shot,
        shot.
You fill the void until last call
at Wagner's Side Door, but it's still
not enough. It's never enough,
so you stumble out to a late night club
with your exes riding your back, one
with hands firmly gripping your wallet, one
flirting with another lifestyle and then
there is the size 2 black dress, the fantasy
friend who cries on your shoulder nightly
over a sleaze ball boyfriend, a minor
leaguer with a girl at home plate for every
away game and you want that, you need that,
but know you can never have it. So you
follow the crowd, swim deeper
into wintering night, switch from gin
to vodka until they throw you out, throw
everyone out, the whole crowd joyfully
creeping down the sidewalk, waiting patiently
at the tracks while a train ratchets by
on riveted rails. You cross the street
to be alone. You want to be gone,
watch the cold steel flat beds pass until
you're standing on top, briefly surfing
the crisp night. You could stay there, escape
to somewhere else, disappear into dark
westbound morning. Instead, you jump,

drop to a cold gravelly ground, a bruised
and broken body falling back to glassy asphalt.
Clouds above lighten with approaching dawn.
You try to move, try to stand, become
someone you imagined in a dream, rise up
from icy pavement on the downhill side
of the tracks and greet a new day.

Morning Rider

You walk your dog before first light,
take him out to do his business.
The growl of a motorcycle engine
intensifies as it draws nearer.
Two heads turn to watch it pass.

Your wife calls it his *squirrel*,
the thing that pulls him out of
whatever obsession he's tracking
whenever you're not home.
She says he's looking for you.

You watch the bike thunder by
in the dark. The timbre of exhaust,
headlight configuration, tell you
what kind of ride it is. It is
5:30 am. You wonder where

this rider is going and think about
your day: Is there a hole in the hedge
of your schedule through which you
could briefly escape, slip away from
this world to explore another?

The dog looks up from the end of the leash.
Perhaps he knows it's not his squirrel
whose rumble now fades in the distance.
Perhaps he too wonders what adventures lie
untethered on the other side of the hedge.

Time and a Half

Stuck behind a man in a white
panel van with aluminum ladders
on top who drives as if he's already
on overtime, creeping up to each light
as if trying to catch it in a butterfly net,
dragging everyone behind him like
a parachute full of time-and-a-half.

Is he daydreaming about how to spend
his new-found excess, the rate of exchange
when he punches in these drawn-out moments
of transportation, time traded for a beverage
at his favorite weekend watering hole, time
traded for the fuel it takes to get him there,
now traded for a cost-accrued *later*
with someone he loves?

There's a phone number on the back door
of the panel van and a question: *How's my driving?*
You want to call that number and tell
whoever answers that his driving is fine
if only he would do it somewhere else.
If only you, too, were eligible for time
and a half on your way to an appointment
for which you are already late.

Sunset Over Suburbia

A hint of color tangles in trees
as the sun falls over the far side
of anonymous rooftops.

Here the last gasp of light
bounces between prefab windows
until all that remains of brick

and siding is muted silhouette.
Soon workers will return home,
close the doors and blinds, confine

the warmth of their lives behind
the silent sameness of this
final destination. For now,

light fades like the muffled voices
of children ending playtime, or
a lonely dog barking, like the whine

of tires swerving toward night
or the clumsy snort of day drifting
into full, indifferent snore.

Driving in the Fog
with Their Headlights Off

Perhaps they don't want to know
which way they're going; don't want
others to know where they've been, don't
want to see or be seen swimming
through pulpy air without the shelter
of stealth, without a gauzy filter
of anonymity. Their silhouettes
approach on the road ahead, haunt
the road behind, guard the mouths
of side streets as if to limit
turn choices for the rest of us.
Phantoms of morning mist, they wait
for nature's veil to cloud a traveler's way;
wait until the playing field
has been leveled to visually-
impaired homogeneity
in which a lack of foresight
becomes an asset, an ally,
a place where everyone dwells
in the same murky delirium.
You can only conclude: They
must be Republicans.

At Bruegger's This Morning

A worker volunteers to wheel
the garbage to the trash bin behind
the building, sneaks a discreet call,
then slips a semi-smart phone back
in the rear pocket of her black stretch pants
where it bulges like a growth throughout
her shift, buzzing occasionally, until
another chance for e-rendezvous
makes her one with the world again.

Four lawyers or real estate mogul
wannabes hold hands and pray over coffee
then discuss developers, contractors,
zoning laws, loopholes and how to get
out from under homeowners' claims
of faulty construction.

Two Meredith College students flitter
in and out, here and there in dirty sneakers,
baggy sweat pants, oversized ball caps.
In line, at tables, over laptops, they check
to see who's watching them. Voyeurs
of another gender, another generation,
you wonder if you appear in their notes
as they do in yours.

The lawyers' conversation shifts
to national politics. It's time for you
to go. Traffic fades on Wade Avenue,
splintering out to daycares, schools,
places of employment.

The *Community Board* on the wall
by the restroom is pinned full
of opportunities. At a restaurant
next door, an NC State flag flaps proudly
in the breeze in this holy, red city.

Upon Cleaning out Your Son's Car

It's not as though you want to buy
his dream car out from under him,
any more than he wants to sell it
to anyone, especially you.

Times being what they are,
the economy being what it is,
child support in arrears, it is
an answer to a dilemma.

Like any good answer
to a financial riddle, it comes
fully equipped with the sucking sound
of someone's wallet being drained.

New tranny, new clutch, new
license plate, insurance, an
assortment of engine lights
clicking off as a checklist of neglect
shrinks down to re-salability
and then he wants to drive it.

As always, you play the bad cop
in his life, the parent who always
says *No.* Justification doesn't matter.
The laws you were scrambling
to stay on the right side of,
don't matter. You've taken
something of his, fixed it,
and denied him access to it.

When you ask him to help clean out
his stuff, to make it ready for sale,
he replies: *It's your car, you clean it.*

So you do.

What was left behind said much about
the previous vehicle owner: seats stained
by careless children, cigar wrappers, a pound
of coins, empty energy drink containers,
assorted unopened legal notices, and two
seven-year-old, un-cashed paychecks.

But the biggest surprise this never-
married father of two left behind
in the console of his car was
a double carton of Trojans.
You admire the optimism, but
wonder what life would be like for him now
if only he had used them years ago.

Hitchhiker

You pick up a hitchhiker in
the parking lot, a little green guy riding
the hood, sunning himself as he creeps
cautiously over a windshield wiper
and higher up the glass.

You expect him to bail the first time
you stop, but he holds the windshield,
climbs higher as you drive, head tilting
curiously, tail waving for balance,
feet fidgeting for better grip.

He reminds you of teenagers
hood-surfing in YouTube videos;
ballsy, acrobatic, wildly stupid,
doing handstands, flips, exhibiting
enduring recklessness of youth.

You drive carefully through traffic,
press the brakes slowly to avoid
a jolt that might send your passenger
tumbling to certain death and wonder
if other drivers can see him bobbing

his head up and down, side to side,
on the glass above your steering wheel.
Would they think he's ornamental?
Wonder if hood surfing had spread
to the animal kingdom?

You park outside a restaurant, expect
your friend to be gone when you return.
Instead he's resting head-downward
on the roof upright, watching. You
reach out a hand to see where he runs.

He lunges forward, lands on your forearm,
scrambles up and over your shoulder, then
launches himself toward a passing car,
a daredevil defying odds, wind,
and consequences to stick the landing.

Note to Self

(for long riders everywhere)

When you see a fire engine
screaming down a nearby onramp,
lights whirling, siren wailing, find
the nearest exit. Never mind if
it drops you on a gravel road
hedged by rows of corn so tall
you can't see anything else,
or dumps you in a dirty, one-
factory town at rush hour, don't
hesitate, escape, nothing good
lies ahead on this soon-to-be
parking lot where something bad
befell someone else. Get off
before lanes become a creeping
procession of gawkers doing
stupid things, before forward
momentum ends in sweltering
stagnation like spit sizzling
to dust on porous asphalt.
Get off before you and your bike
in bumper to bumper become
a roasting party, basting you
in your own brine.

Riding with the Valkyries

For Joe and Mark

More than twenty-five years
in North Carolina and you've never ridden
a motorcycle on the Blue Ridge Parkway
until a rainy day in June when you join
a clutch of riders on Honda Valkyries
seeking glory above and beyond.
Dodging downbursts on slick asphalt
you whip through thickening fog
toward the top of Mt. Mitchell,
you on a Harley sandwiched
between two Valkyries,
a hint of Wagner opera
climaxing your ascent,
Elmer Fudd directing
the procession, Bugs Bunny
riding wise guy, a cast of demons
silhouetted against the dreary skyline
as you wind steadily upward, your escorts
and you disappearing into mist-darkened heavens.

St. Jill of Albion

True love rides behind you in rain gear
from Pittsburgh to Deep Creek Lake, Maryland
through late June monsoon and doesn't complain.

She warms your back on the way down, laughs
when you arrive drenched and muddy, then
wrings water from your socks and riding jersey.

Fourteen riders signed up for this trip,
fourteen experienced bikers, but
only you, Joe, and Sumo showed and rode

and then there was the lady on the back
of your bike, the one who hates mud, shivers
when air dips below sixty-five degrees,

the one who unpacked a spare pair of jeans
and sweatshirt before you left to fit
a curling iron and blow dryer in your bag.

Your hosts are in awe of this woman
who your own family proclaims a saint
for putting up with your shenanigans.

But there's so much more to the story:
outracing funnel clouds in central
Nebraska, driving a Crown Vic through

Rabbit Ears Pass during a white out,
skating black ice in West Virginia at
seventy and only clipping a guard rail.

She threatened to let Texas cops keep you
when their lights lit up as you passed going
one-ten in the other direction.

And who can forget that shortcut
around Mt. Hood when an accident
closed highway 35? You rerouted

to a country road on your Gazetteer
that degraded to misty logging trail
at 10K feet in Big Foot country.

She's traveled too many roads with you
to panic when you live too fast for
conditions, conditions come and go,

and still you manage, you adapt, you
move on, you and your companion,
navigating these roads together.

On the Road to Weymouth

September 15, 2012

You set out in morning darkness, witness
the sun rise over the rolling road ahead.
Hues of pink and purple spread across
the sky, highlight mist-covered fields
and fog stuffed like wads of cotton candy
into low-lying country pockets.

Braced against the wind of passage,
blasts that hit you head-on as you ride,
a crosswind would sometimes catch the bike
and buck you sideways unexpected.

Your head fills with the hum
of wheels, a fragrant brew of car exhaust,
dewy dampness from fresh-cut fields,
warm manure and a whole variety
of roadside rot, as you rumble down
route 24/27 considering
your obituary.

You lost a friend two weeks ago,
a fellow poet who died too young.
Last week another friend's wife called
to say his mind had drifted beyond the buoy,
past the point where he could carry on
a conversation.

The roadside gullies are filled
with travel debris. One good gust,
a sudden stop by a careless driver
and that could be you.

You stop at a Waffle House
in the middle of nowhere.
Who puts a Waffle House here?
And who are these people who find it,
fill it with chattering tourists
in travel pajamas the color
of their favorite football team?

The waitress keeps your coffee hot
as you wait for a plate of bacon, eggs and grits.
You used to snicker when folks ordered grits,
dragging the vowel sound out an extra beat.
You were a Yankee then. You didn't do *gr-e-i-ts*.
You don't know what you are now.

You've been in Carolina so long
your feet feel like clay-covered stumps.
You still display a *Steeler* logo everywhere you go,
but there's always been a little *Tarheel*
in your heart. You wonder if loyalties
such as these are nostalgia or whims
of circumstance and whether anyone will
claim you when your final words are written.

II. TRAVELERS

Roadside Fantasies

He likes the way she touches
everything with her mouth, licks
the salt on his shoulder, rips
a plastic bag with her teeth, catches
snowflakes on her tongue, nibbles
on babies' fingertips, bites her nails.

But none of it matters. It's all
road mirage, memories of interactions
that never happened, never will.

He's on a fuel break at a pit stop
beside a highway of strangers heading
in different directions. Alone
on a motorcycle with no radio,
no companion, his eyes rest on
whoever crosses his line of sight,
contemplate this randomness, this
almost meeting, reinvent the un-
remarkable as a means to pass the time.

Second Skin

You see him everywhere, wearing
a Harley T-shirt to ride a bicycle.
One day crimson, the next yellow,
another day traffic cone orange.
You wonder if his apparel helps
his legs pump longer, ache less.
Does he pedal to the rhythm
of a running engine, move faster,
slice the wind more cleanly?
Does he wear them to remind
himself where the heart of two-
wheeling is rooted? Or is it
a message to others; a caution
flag for the less attentive, how
this rider reveals a split
personality? A second skin like
a brightly colored snake or insect,
a hint of hidden danger, a sign
something venomous lurks within?

Exposing the Goods

Surely the man who jogs Main St.
every morning during rush hour
feels healthy and satisfied, but
all we see is gender-defying
man-boobs bouncing with a jolt
from each foot fall, an impact
rippling through his body like
a tsunami trying to wash
away a lifetime of listlessness.
We want to tell him: *It isn't*
working neighbor, ask him
if he's ever considered
testosterone injections
or surgery, remind him
that buses truck children
to school each day on this road
and while their impressionable
eyes are barely open at 7am,
a heavier shirt, a strap, hell,
even a bra might shield them
from a lifetime of confusion.

Relentless

(In line at the Post Office)

Relentless it said in bold script,
hip-high across her lower back,
embellished with loops and curves.
Nice art adorning an even nicer canvas.

A rose garnished the back of her hand,
a mural on her left shoulder
brandished the words *Carpe Diem*.
Surely no one who left the house

in low-hung pajama bottoms,
a pink bra shouting out from underneath
a sheer white spaghetti-strap top,
scissor-cropped just below her breasts,

surely no one with fuchsia hair,
dressed and painted so alluringly
would begrudge his gaze or chastise him
for scribbling mental notes. After

the first smack, we all enter the world
in costume, some to stay anonymous,
some to scream in their bravest voice,
Here I am world. As she flip-flops toward

the door, he wonders what thorns
shadow a woman who seizes the day
relentlessly, who blushes brightly against
gray petals in a sun-bleached garden.

Posterboy

He painted his truck black,
flat black, chalkboard black,
so he could share the wealth
of his wisdom with the world.

One day a Bible verse,
the next a cut out catchphrase from
the Constitution or Bill of Rights.
Sometimes both share space on

a tailgate, door or quarter panel;
his best Moses, John, or Jerry Falwell
impersonations intertwined with variations
on notes from forefathers and patriots

like Timothy McVeigh and Ted Kaczinski.
The gospel of rebellion, rolling down the road,
all four wheels firmly grounded in the faith
of his own righteousness, simultaneously

proclaiming *He has Risen, The 2nd
Amendment makes all others possible,*
and *Same sex marriage is BLASPHEMY.* Today
he pulls into the lot, parks across three spaces

with Hank Williams, Jr. riding shotgun
at 90 decibels, *Obama is the Anti-Christ*
sketched on his passenger door and all we
can do is pray for much-needed rain.

Highway Man

He sees himself as a road warrior,
not a Mad Max post-apocalyptic mercenary type,
but someone who drives angry,
drives with a vengeance,
drives determined to arrive on time.
He wants a road to call his own,
free from the scourge of soccer mom
minivans drifting in and out of lanes
between cell phone calls, free
from overcautious octogenarians
in thirty-year-old Le Sabres, free
from truckers side-by-side, holding hands
and skipping uphill as they haul oversized loads;
free from entitlement Caddys and crotch rockets
that slash across multiple lanes like rash
hummingbirds, disrupting the bubble
of space he clears for himself against
an erratic shamble of traffic.
It's all very simple to him:
drive it or park it, but stay
the hell out of his way.
There is *Point A* and *Point B*
and no point obstructing the distance between,
no point debating right-of-way or speed.
All he wants is room to ride, wheels
to carry him, fuel to burn, and time.
Everything else is scenery or obstacle.

At McDonald's Near Rocky Top

You watch a trucker climb down from his rig
    as if he were climbing off a stagecoach
and wonder if much has changed since then
    for guys like him who spend long hours

on hard seats surrounded by melo-
    dramatic motorists whose greatest fear
is being trapped behind a guy like him
    on the downhill side of an uphill climb.

People who curse the lumbering
    awkwardness, lane space consumption,
the thick cloud of diesel exhaust
    or sweet ratcheting smell of burning brakes

left in his wake. What would they say
    if they saw this driver as you do now,
climbing carefully down, trudging toward
    the door of a restaurant, his back

and shoulders rounded, his gait ragged
    from screaming knee joints? Would they
see an ex-athlete, a wounded warrior,
    or a man who wears his age like a stained

and tattered T-shirt hanging over
    a settled mass of ballooning miles,
more miles than they may ever know?
    You exchange nods as you mount your bike.

A Harley cap on his head says he's
   a fellow rider and you wonder what joy
he'd find cruising these same roads on a sticky
   leather seat with hot steel between his legs.

Order of the Day

He wears yesterday's Happy Meal to brunch.
She arrives at his table all white
polyester and red cotton apron
and moves as if she spent the night dancing
with prescription bottle castanets.

He looks for a sapphire seed of hope,
a black pearl, in the swollen caverns
of her eyes, but it's all darkness there.

When she speaks, "What can I get you, Hon?"
falls like blank verse from her lips and he knows
he wants nothing to do with her soap opera life,
doesn't want to be a long distance voyeur
skimming through disaster scenes as they unfold.

It's almost noon and the moon still
hangs like a crescent-shaped omen
against a promising blue sky,
but he knows she'll never see it.

He knows she has a husband or boyfriend
and three kids. They always do. He always
knows. Her silence dampens the drama,
a plot with many holes, minor nuances,
a penchant for the traumatic.

She finally returns and drops
a chattering coffee cup on his table.
He senses a storm of tears not far
ahead and proceeds to tell her
he likes his home fries extra crispy.

Flag Waving
(July 4, 2015)

Independence Day in Summersville,
West Virginia finds *The Blob* wedged
between the seat and steering wheel
of a red Chevy truck jacked up so high
he must have needed a ladder or crane
or a crew with ropes and pulleys to lift
him into place so he could parade down
the main road of this pass-through town
with a 6-foot flag propped in the bed
of his pick-up, flapping in the breeze;
a NASCAR cap crowning his bubble head,
as he bounces to the rhythm of pot-
holes and road roughage.

Is it an act of defiance, choosing
this day to flaunt the stars and bars
of another time, another country?
Does he truly believe his heritage
is under assault or is this a demon-
stration of solidarity with white
supremacists or a mass murderer
in South Carolina? Does he realize
the irony of his actions: Flying
a flag of rebellion, the flag of a beaten
nation, in the only state to rebel
against the rebels, the only state
to secede from the Confederacy?

Check, Please

He imagines a conversation with
the whistler at the table beside him.
It would start something like this:
"Has anyone ever asked you
to stop whistling before?"

If the answer is, "No," he would say,
"Welcome to a new experience."
If the answer is, "Yes," perhaps
a smile, a raised eyebrow, a wink
or puckered lips will do.

What if the parents of the child parked
in the booth behind him don't believe
in discipline? Don't believe a toddler
can misbehave? Think padded seats
were designed for jumping?

He may be forced to forego that slice
of Aunt Jane's Famous Apple Pie—
a la mode, of course.

Across the diner a young Mom pours
apple juice in a cup for her son. It looks
like urine and he feels an urge to piss.

Through a window he watches one truck
roll out as another rig lurches to a stop.
The pumps are a mob of minivans
and SUVs with roof racks full of luggage
or kayaks, pulling pop ups or trailers.

Everybody's going somewhere,
chance found them all here at this time,
this place, but it's not his place and he
doesn't want their time to infringe on his own,
doesn't want to go where they're going.

He apologizes to Aunt Jane, thanks
his waitress, requests his check and leaves,
unsure of his next destination, unsure
where this road might end, but certain
he'll go anyway. He always does,
if only to see what's over the next hill.

The Body of Her Work
after SW

She's obsessed with bodies,
her body, her partner's body,
anybody, a body of work about
bodies, colliding, changing,
longing to mingle with other
bodies, to swim a sea of other
bodies, become other bodies,
to find somebody to prove
nobody can deny a body for
what it is; for what it wants
to be, nobody owns the patent,
the recipe for right body versus
wrong body, for him versus her,
nobody is immune
to loneliness rooted
in solemn corners of every
body, yours, mine, theirs, hers,
foreign as it is, unwelcome
as it is, unacceptable as it is,
it is undeniably her body, an anti-
body in a sea of somebodies,
wholly connected and detached
from a greater body by
a prankster god who gifted her
this life, this body to which she clings
relentlessly unrepentant, still
wishing she could make him
take it back.

Selfie-Absorbed

Her voyage of selfie-discovery
begins by posting each day's agenda
online: tutor today, volunteer
tomorrow at a local pet clinic.

Each requires a different fashion
statement and bright is her favorite form
of selfie-expression, this forum
a daily boost of selfie-esteem.

But she must refresh her selfie-image
often: today's lunch date, dinner later
with Mr. Right (to-be), an errand to
the neighborhood grocery store—

All so compelling, so selfie-aware.
We need to know what brands she buys, which route
she takes, her parking woes, the creeps who hang out
at the mall and look at her,   *look* at her.

Each post designed to keep the regulars
tuned in, a minute-by-minute update,
her own reality show. She invites
new friends to peer through the pane at her life:

She's selfie-employed, a single mom whose
selfie-reliance depends on the traffic
of others. Red lips, a coy smile, vivid blush,
radical eye liner, and a tight top

to squeeze everything into proper
perspective, a straight line that misses
the heart of the matter: a shortage
of selfie-control, selfie-respect.

Insufficiently selfie-sufficient,
a lack of selfie-discipline attracts
the darker side of e-friendships: dick pics
and propositions arrive by private message,

provoke a selfie-righteous response, but
no selfie-inspection, no selfie-doubt
that she's the victim of perverse others
and not participant, provocateur.

She's invisible in a selfie-less world,
a master at the art of selfie-denial,
but knows her place in cyberspace, knows
the social network pecking order, lets

this selfie madness feed upon itself
by keeping herself at arm's length.

Emoji This

He doesn't speak emoji, doesn't replace
perfectly good words with cartoons, swap
phrases for linguistic avatars, hieroglyphs
for future beings to translate back to
the language from which they sprang.
He can do without pop culture cutesiness,
electronic doodlings of a bored generation
aspiring to leave its mark on history
through frivolous fingertip tapping.
He likes the curve of letters, the bark
of consonants, the visual rhythm
of antiquated syllables stumbling
over cobbled substrates. He imagines
a stray text or email bouncing off
a satellite. Caught by solar wind,
it pinballs through the cosmos
to become humanity's first contact
with otherworldly beings. Will they
recognize a string of yellow smiley faces
as shorthand for more evolved language,
a dispatch worthy of further study?
Or will they see shredded fragments
of literacy, scribblings of a long dead
minor world, flatulence vented
to the eternal void, little more
than cosmic noise, interstellar spam
to file in a galactic recycle bin?

Drive Through

On a slow day at the drive through,
he shares two cigarettes with the lady
in the car ahead of him, each drag
a reminder of another lifetime,
another vice from which he'd escaped.
He could close his window, seal the odor out,
but it's seventy-five degrees in February,
a muted sun is warming winter rot,
this scented siren beckoned him
from the side of the road. It's 10am
on Tuesday. Breakfast is a memory
fluttering from the corner of a dark
morning meeting miles away. He was
heading back to the office when
Chick-fil-a ambushed him, dragged him
nose first to the drive-through line where
flight is not an option, trapped between
the order kiosk and satisfaction
he inhales the smell of progress, creeps
toward the check-out window: chicken
and biscuits, coffee and Marlboro Lights,
thankful that the line, now wrapped
around the building, didn't park him
beside the dumpster.

Jack & Julie

Julie nurses a wound so dark
even Jesus can't find her with the light
of salvation, still she remains

faithful as husband, Jack,
tries to wash away her worries
with glasses of Chardonnay.

He matches her consumption
two for one with bottles of Bud,
spinning yarns to anyone

who'll listen, but mostly her. He wants
to free her from the funk that chains
her heart, entertain her, seduce her,

revive the girl he married, the one
in the flowered sundress he brought
through the door an hour before,

but she's not falling for his act
again. She touches a crucifix
that hangs from her neck and reaches

across the meeting bar to the arm
of a stranger, lays out a case against
her man, against his public charm,

her private prison. She longs for
a kindred spirit to liberate her,
help her grieve and leave, start over

by ending this cruel charade, seeks
someone to witness her sorrow,
shoulder the weight of her burden.

Instead she finds another wall,
another vacuous male accomplice
to her misery, a godless nonbeliever

who has seen deep-seated sorrow
before, recognizes her dark
addiction to tragedy, drama,

a needfulness he knows no one
can satisfy—least of all him—knows
it's time for him to move along.

He imparts his best barroom wisdom,
shakes Jack's hand, tells them both he's going
outside to smoke, hears her mutter

to Jack as he heads for the door, "I just
want to leave, just want to get the fuck out,"
and he hopes they do before he returns.

Pegged

"Sometimes you've got more balls than brains."
                        —William H. Douglass, Jr.

He always wanted highway pegs
on his motorcycle; flat chrome-plated
ones that fold up when not in use,
lined with black rubber runners
to keep his feet from slipping off.

He hasn't bought them yet because
they're not practical for the places
he usually rides, stoplight-obsessed
city streets and winding country roads,
but it doesn't make him want them any less.

It's an image thing.

He sees himself ripping down the road, pegs
angled so the wind blows up his pant legs.
He's cool all under and doesn't care
if his riding position resembles
a woman, feet in stirrups, giving birth.

That's not the message he wants to convey
to fellow travelers. He wants them to see him
as a man who isn't afraid to ride
the fast lane, isn't afraid to rush out
into the world and greet it balls first.

Harmless

She tells her girlfriend, "Some harmless old guy,"
when asked about the man she squiggled
across the room to press herself against.
"He's usually good for a drink or two."

He's seen this scene play out before, the same
flirtatious mockery, the same phrase hung
around some guy's neck like an ID card
or convention badge that says the wearer

is a member of an exclusive club,
a fraternity of friendlies, *safe*.
It says something about that man when
a woman can casually press the goods

against him and walk away rewarded
for a moment's lease, his name lost amid
the multitude of others she sees
as marks, as if the words *USE ME* were taped

to the back of a shirt or tattooed
across a forehead. *Harmless*, first cousin
to *helpless*; a cat declawed, a bee without
a stinger, a label he vows will never
cast its shadow over him.

Poetry Reading at a Biker Bar

Jessica's got it all going on; all
the curves in all the right places
and fabric stretched to emphasize
and expose. She steps to the mike,
lowers it, holds it in her hands in a way
that demands every man's full attention.
Her voice oozes dark and low
from prurient lips. She rides the mike
stand like a practiced pole dancer,
a restrained rhythm rises to meet
a climax of words. The split seams
of her jeans struggle to contain
soft thighs that flex to escape.
We watch spellbound, drips
of sweat kissing our cheeks
on this sultry night as her words
vanish like whispered breaths
in a steamy shower. We want
to let them shimmy down over us,
drench us in lyrical enlightenment
but that's not what this poem is about
now is it?

III. THE ROAD ITSELF

Kickstand Up

When the kickstand is up, it's time to roll.
A weekend warrior rally will do, complete
with poker chips and coffee stops every
fifty miles or so, but it's really not your style.

That's a parade, a social event,
a fashion show for customized street steel,
not the right scene for a rider who likes
to take the long road, favors the throttle
wide open, wants to run full out until
the tank runs dry, a rider who needs
to consume endless stretches of asphalt.

This revelation comes to you later
in life than most, color bleached from your hair,
your beard, but not your heart. A mileage
deficiency fueling this urge to ride,
to catch the pack around the corner,
over the hill, to chase yesterday's sun
with today still nipping at your heels.

Westbound

You roll out early, hoping to beat
rush hour traffic. The rear windows
of vehicles you pass reflect pink
and purple layers of sunrise.
At a bottleneck, a family van driver
in the lane next to you gazes at luggage
strapped to the passenger seat of your
motorcycle. You hear her heart wonder
if this is freedom and how it feels.

> In this fantasy, you answer:
> *Come. Ride with me. Feel rain*
> *and sand sting your cheeks*
> *at seventy miles an hour, taste*
> *tire dust and sprayed blood*
> *from suicidal insects, savor*
> *the many flavors of road rot,*
> *decay, death; show me your body*
> *can handle ten hours in the saddle*
> *then we'll talk about freedom,*
> *we'll talk about a love so strong*
> *it aches for more aches.*

The highway splits as the sun breaches
low-hanging clouds, warms your back.
A halo appears in front of you,
around a shadow of your head: light
refracting through your windshield,
illuminating the road itself, as if
to highlight a passage in the book
of the open road, reveal a sacred
path to another wayward spirit.

Crossing Tennessee

From Knoxville to Nashville, one minute
a scorching hell, the next a fire hose,
a waterfall, a spray of icy BBs.

You remember a rest stop near Cookeville,
a young girl—maybe nineteen—hunkered
at a picnic table under concrete awning.

Barely dressed, shivering, she started
a "where you from" conversation. She
was from Clarksburg, West Virginia, until

you said you'd been there. Then silence.
It didn't cross your mind at the time
that she was a hooker, or the thirty-

year-old Oldsmobile with the wide
back seat was her office; never
occurred to you that you had breached

her workspace or the person flashing
headlights from behind her office
steering wheel was a pimp. You only

stopped seeking shelter from the hail,
to adjust rain gear, drink water, and check
cell phone, email, text messages.

But you understand how hard it is to run
a business from the side of the road.
You roll past the foggy Olds as you leave,

consider financial feasibility here
in the middle of Tennessee nowhere,
one road access, and poor cellular reception.

Kentucky Rising

Nothing compares to the smell of manure
stewing in mid-morning sun. A day after

monsoons have passed, hills are neon:
alive, awake, and sponging what remains.

Nothing is the same as a vacant stretch
of road rolling silent and gray ahead

as if it were built for you and you alone,
a private passageway, a corridor

cutting across Kentucky back country
from Bowling Green to Owensboro.

Wind rushing past your ears muffles the sound
of your engine, of tires being chewed

by asphalt, dissolving into its skin
like rain into parched earth or blue sky

melting down to a muddy horizon.
Up ahead the road merges, intersects,

or ends. They all do one or the other.
Traffic will replace wet shit with exhaust,

budding trees with neon fast food signs.
Nothing to write home about, but you will

remember this trip and keep it with you
after the final grains of rubber dust

have been washed from your clothes, your hair, your beard,
long after you've parked your bike forever

and the road has forgotten you, your
journeys, how well you wore your wheels.

Rain

It changes everything,
dust and pollen coalesce
to a slick slurry, dry leaves
transform to slimy salad.
It's Nature's way of cleansing
these ugly gray ribbons
that slice across her body,
her means of sanitizing
everything, including you.
Watch the sky for warning signs,
approach each bend as if
gyroscopic force, that fragile
cosmic law, that friend you must
rely upon to spring you upright
in leaner curves, as if it
has deserted you, left behind
a souvenir, a jilted lover
whose toxic tears saturate
your every destination,
unforgettable as a woman,
inescapable as road hazard.

Rush Hour on the 465 Beltway the Morning After Tornados Pass Through

It's not a sneer, a growl, a threat
of aggression pasted on the face
of the biker you pass on this racetrack
around Indianapolis.   It's
the stoic calm of a rider focused
on finessing damp roads, misty air,
abrupt wind shifts and a surging
sea of metal-jacketed chaos,
wave after wave of coffee-sipping,
smart phone obsessed commuters weaving
their way to work, across narrow lanes,
around orange cones, construction barrels,
a flood of drones draining toward a hub
of perceived security, braiding
an ever-thickening rope
to strangle traffic, dam the flow
at every junction and in the middle
of this madness a rider holds his line
against the mania that tries
to drag him down with the weight
of its undertow.

Long Rider

Act 1

After dodging two tornados on the way into Chicago,
the city waves a gusty goodbye and blows you back
the way you came with another storm barking up
your backside and a warning: *Don't slow down
until you pass Indianapolis.*

You shoot the gaps between the moving canyons
of swaying semis until road widening on I-65
narrows lanes, compresses traffic to a crawl
with a purple wall of weather closing in.

> *You remember an accident near Cincinnati
> on the trip up, two hours, six miles of stop
> and go, still in rain gear after rain had stopped,
> sweating, gauging the wide center berm, whether
> anyone would mind if you made like the EVs
> that already passed and evade that parking lot.
> How two bikers cruising by rescued you from
> indecision as you fell in behind them
> and three riders skirted and wove along
> the side of the road, crossed over the exit detour
> and on to freedom north of the calamity.*

When the first stings of rain spritz your cheek, you slide
into the rough on the right, cruise slowly by. Eight
miles later, the highway opens, but the dark clouds
you've watched in your mirrors are now on top
of you. You stop beneath a bridge abutment, don
a full-face helmet, change gloves.

Cars you passed in the construction zone catch up.
Before, some had honked, flashed the finger, a few
threw bottles as you broke away, leaving them trapped.
Now a karmic glow brightens their faces:
satisfied smiles accompany sardonic waves.

The next sixty miles are like that. You stop once
to refuel, then a restroom break, and once more
when the rain is too heavy to see the road.
You hear the voice of a friend ask: *Why ride instead*
of flying, instead of driving in a perfectly good car
with a roof, doors, and windows?

You know she's right. It would be easier, more
comfortable. You wouldn't need special gear
to drive your truck, no bag to protect your clothes
and valuables. Your hands and crotch would stay dry,
and windshield wipers, what a concept.

Some people will never understand: You're here
by choice, a challenge of sorts, a gauntlet
the road itself slaps you with each time
you roll out to a new destination.

The day will come when you're forced
to park your wheels like a museum display,
remember the roads, the scenery,
the strangers you met along the way.

Until then, each minute is a bonus
you pay yourself in accrued time,
a benefit earned through labor,
the economics of leisure no one
gets to define for you.

Twenty miles north of Lafayette,
lightning strikes so close to the road you feel
the static sting of discharge, feel rolling rumbles
vibrate through your wheels. A curled edge of light
behind you signals the storm's end is near, but when
you stop, it stops, keeping pace with your progress.
You know then you'll never outrun it, never reach
the other side of Indianapolis tonight.

Three miles north of Lafayette, vehicles
have hydroplaned off the road. A two-hour
segment of your journey has now been stretched
to five. You concede you've had enough rain,
put in at the next exit, your front wheel
plowing through road pond, a v-shaped wave
sizzling against your engine's underside.

Act 2

The Quality Inn has a bad vibe, but you've
stayed in worse, so you slosh into the lobby
in full gear, making a watery comfort zone
between you and others also seeking refuge.

The guy behind the counter resembles
a front man for a grunge band in black
sleeveless tee, tattoos, and pierced studs
like those on your saddlebags. A young girl,
maybe ten, maybe his daughter, walks up
in a dress similar to the one worn by
the twins in *The Shining*. She asks if you
ride a moped. You tell her *something like that*
as dad sends her after a mop and bucket.

This place is her home, her playground.
You see her often during your brief stay,
coming and going in the hall or elevator,
sometimes just standing, watching, watching.

As you unload your gear, you notice
a spotter in a second floor window —
the room above the entranceway.
There are no blinds and it's all steamed over
except for a circular spot wiped clean,
head high to anyone seated there.

Another guy in a ball cap and work shirt
with torn sleeves circles the building twice
in an old blue pickup, leaning out, scanning
the upper floors. You carry your bags
to a third-floor room and wonder if this hotel
is just a hub of weirdness or something worse.

On your way to pick up dinner, you pass
the laundry room on the second floor.
A skinny shirtless twenty-something pokes
his head out of a door, looks right first then left,
sees you, curses, ducks back in, slams the door.
Not who he was expecting you think.

Once a guest room, the converted laundry
holds one washer and one dryer—both full.
You'll check again after eating.
Down the hall a woman in a short,
loosely-tied silk robe leaves one room,
crosses the hall, enters another.

You walk to Subway, fetch dinner, come back
to find a cop car blocking the entrance, EMTs
in the doorway, and two bald white guys
facing off in the parking lot, talking softly,
making vague gestures toward the scene.

The driver of the rusty truck must have
done something foolish, but he's in the wind.
Time seems frozen as you enter.
No one talks. No one moves. No one
stops you, asks questions, offers explanation.
It's like a routine day for these people.

The dryer is empty when you pass. You rush
to your room, grab a pile of damp clothes, coins,
return to the second floor, load them, wait.
The squirrelly guy across the hall opens
his door again, sees you. Eyes full of panic,
he nearly closes the door on his hand.

Nuts is your first thought, followed by *junkie*
as a portrait of this place begins to unfold.
His must be the room above the entranceway.
He's *the lookout*. In his mind, in this world, *you*
are a person of concern, a misfit.

Soon a gangly kid with greasy hair, ragged jeans,
and ball cap turned backwards, comes to the door
with a short round girl stuffed in her younger
sister's clothes. *Squirrel* tells them to get in quick
and close the door. They shuffle in with no shared
sense of urgency and leave the door unlatched.

You hear them talk. *The Squirrel* is scared.
Then the shorter of the two bald guys
from the parking lot arrives, doesn't knock,
bangs the door open, then closed. A muffle
of loud chatter seeps through the hollow door,
then silence, then the door reopens, the bald guy
struts across the hall and straight for you.

He plants himself in front of you, looks across you
as if addressing something on the wall behind,
asks a question, "Why does Tim have to go with you?"

His right hand is propped behind his hip where you know
he hides a fist or maybe something more lethal.
You know now who this guy is, his function here.
He's an enforcer, at least twenty years younger
than you, built like all the catchers you've known—
not over-muscled, but strong, poised to strike
if he doesn't like your answer.

You don't move, never look away, focus
on the caterpillar surfing his upper lip,
the way his mouth twitches as he speaks.
He's stiff as stone, but smells like fear.
The second floor is his turf, his domain.
Timmy the Squirrel works for him
and you are interfering with commerce.

"Who the hell is Tim?" you ask and watch
tension drain from his shoulders. He turns,
looks directly at you for the first time,
"You're just here doing laundry?"
"Just doing laundry, chief" you say,
but as he stomps away you think about Tim,
how he put you in the middle of his business,
and add, "I think someone's fucking with you."

He thinks so, too. First there's shouting,
then silence, then Tim is rag-dolled
around the room, apologizing, pleading.

Four people are in that room. If someone
gets stupid, a weapon comes out, you're in
a likely line of fire. You open the dryer,
decide slightly damp and alive beats
totally dry and bloody every time.
You gather your things, leave
the second floor to itself, go back
to your room and plan an early escape.

Epilogue

The alarm sounds at 4:25, but you're
already awake, watching patterns
of light dance on your ceiling, reflecting
from an ambulance below. You're sure
they've come for Tim and probably not
the first time, suspect the Quality Inn
is a regular stop for the night shift.

You pass the taller of the two bald guys
on your way out, bags in hand, and figure
they, too, must work in shifts. This one's built
like a linebacker, formidable, but only glances
at you, offers a nod like another biker might
if you met at a traffic light.

No free breakfast here, you roll out
in misty, damp pre-dawn Indiana,
hoping to clear the beltway before
Monday morning commuters wake
and clutter your route.

You think about Tim as you go, if it was him
they hauled away this morning. Part of you
feels bad about the beating you know he took.
Part of you believes he deserved it for dumping
the sum of his sins on a stranger.

You're not expecting rain today so you wear
light rain gear and half-shell helmet. It's dark,
but the sun will be up soon. You slide your
sunglasses on, fall in behind long haulers
and early commuters using taillights
for guidance and distance, remain alert,
vigilant, well aware that road hazards can
materialize at any time, in many forms.

Skirting St. Louis

Your day starts in Kentucky, early
in Kentucky. You like early, you like
Kentucky and still you leave it
hanging like laundry left on a line

in a cloud burst, evacuate as if
yesterday's rains were still chasing you,
threatening to drain you downstream
and dump you in the Ohio River

with all the other gutter trash
that washes up later on a muddy
Indiana shore where you don't
stay long, either. You're only

passing through, cutting corners,
on the way to somewhere else.
Next stop: Mt. Vernon, Illinois,
a lunch and refueling break.

The Rt. 15 strip near Mt. Vernon
reminds you of Monroeville's Miracle Mile:
fast food heaven sandwiched between
an interstate and small town U-S-A.

No one's in a hurry here, no one cares
if you're riding two wheels or pulling
eighteen. Until harvest, you are the crop
that pays the bills and buys the beer.

No GPS on the bike, so you check
your map, see that north to Champaign
then west is longer than skirting St. Louis.
It's 2pm. You wonder if you can beat

rush hour traffic but know, if you don't,
six hours of riding on a black
leather saddle in afternoon sun—
sweat, a layer of honey between

clothes and skin—will be like spring dew.
Still you bet on the shortest route, sprint
across the Mississippi, eye empty
downtown parking decks at 4pm.

Your gut tells you something's wrong,
twists into knots like constricting traffic,
all ten lanes become impassable wall,
a crawling tour of St. Louis beltway.

You're off-course on a motorbike,
trapped in traffic in scorching heat—
an all too familiar recipe. Now cook
two hours uncovered between exits,

air heavy and sweet as burnt sugar,
asphalt percolating through the soles
of your boots, engine–baked thighs
screaming for relief as your fuel gauge

tips toward bad news for you, the middle
sardine in a cramped can that stretches
from guardrail to guardrail from here to
the outer limits of suburbia.

Free at last, somewhere north of Wentzville,
you feed the bike four gallons of gas, drink
two bottles of water yourself, squeeze
a melted power bar into your mouth.

There is still light left to burn and time
to be recovered from today's miscue.
You think about the road not taken
and wonder where you'd be right now

if you had. You know that road.
It's why you chose this road, why you
often choose one road over another.
A green sign at the end of the onramp

says sixty-eight miles to Hannibal.
You've never been to Hannibal, sounds
new, historic, adventurous, sounds like
a road that could make all the difference.

When You Think of Hannibal, MO

You think of Mark Twain, Tom Sawyer,
life on a river. Reality sometimes muddies
the waters of boyhood misconceptions.
Tom and Huck knew that. You discover it
anew on your way through. You wanted
to stay here, but recognized right away
this remake of a B Western. Some
of the props have been updated, but a cowboy
is a cowboy, is a cowboy, and you've seen
their brand of folk before. They may have traded
buckboards for mud-runners, spurs for steel toes,
but the plot remains the same: *wild boys come out to play
when the sun goes down.* Tonight they're racing mudder trucks
with four-foot tires and short exhausts down Main Street;
revving engines, popping clutches, lurching at street lights —
country music and smudged ball caps all around.
At one stoplight, a pack of ATVs comes out
of nowhere, flies across the intersection,
the rear rider's front wheels raised high above
the road like a rearing bronco. You wonder how
he steers that thing, but know you don't want to be
wherever he's going, know Sam Clemens would have
written this story different. If he was dealt this hand,
he might have played it out just to watch the drama
unfold, but you've seen this scene before and know
a losing hand when you hold it, so you fold
and hope you're dealt a better one
up the road, across the river.

Finding Iowa

You don't like to ride at night when
bugs are bigger, people dumber.
You remember a night ride years
ago from Findley Lake to Erie.
A June Bug kissed your forehead
at sixty-five miles an hour and
nearly knocked you off the bike.

You come to Iowa late, but
sunlight angling across the road
says there's still light left to wring
from the day and cool evening air
is a comforting contrast
to blistering St. Louis traffic.

Somewhere ahead you will park
for the night, unhitch the dry bag
you bungied to your seat, drag it
to a dark room and crank the AC.
But you haven't found that exit yet.

The ramp for Mt. Pleasant loops around
enough land to grow corn for a third
world nation and ends at a road sign
with two arrows: one for Mt. Pleasant,
the other for Ottumwa to which
your mind attaches the subtext:
Home of Radar O'Reilly and you
wonder about a town that owes
its fame to a fictional character.

A herd of hotels huddle here
like bison on a winter prairie.
The Best Western is out front like
an old bull, its lot full of RVs
and pickups—some parked on the grass.

A guy in a John Deere cap sits on
the front lawn in a green and white
folding chair made of woven
nylon mesh. In one hand he holds
a 2-liter bottle of Coke,
in the other a spatula
to flip the burger he's cooking
on a mini charcoal grill.

You decide to pass on the Best
Western, imagine bonfires
and pistol popping might also
be part of the evening agenda—
not the ambience you desire.

A Comfort Inn is tucked behind it.
You roll up beneath the awning,
park and drag a numb leg over
your leather saddle, shake it back
to life as you walk to the lobby.

No one is manning the counter
at 8pm. You holler but no one
replies. Tap the bell and notice
a commotion in the breakfast
area: a swarm of seniors.
Maybe someone there can help me,
you think, then turn back to the desk,
startled to find someone standing there.

You ask for a room and she says,
"Aw, hon, there ain't a room around
for a hundred miles, but I could
get you something in Iowa City."
Iowa City, another
two hours of highway riding.

You thank her, decline the offer,
and turn to the door. You'll call your wife,
have her book a room for you somewhere,
but before you leave you turn back
to the clerk with an urgent need to know:
   why here, why so many people stopped
   at this tiny dot on the map?

You ask, she answers, "Oh, honey,
there's a big tractor pull tomorrow,"
and you realize you have entered
the *Twilight Zone*, another dimension
of space and time in a parallel universe
where vocation and recreation
have somehow become confused.

You call home to another time zone,
wake your wife, ask her to find you
something cheap, easy to locate
in the dark, climb back on the bike,
back onto the highway, head north
into darkening Iowa night, where
a faint scent of shit paints the air
as the sun slides away, revealing
a world you never knew existed.

First Impressions

North Carolina and Virginia sneak by
in morning dark. You're barely awake when
West Virginia gives way to southern Ohio
where fragile farmland beside the highway
is brittle-brown and whistles in the wind.

The elevator at the Best Western
in Indiana smells like old mop,
your room smells like antiseptic, you
smell like the road residue that sticks
to your skin where you lathered on sun screen.

Your pants walk themselves to a corner,
collapse exhausted in a heap. Tomorrow
they will crawl back up your calves and thighs
and cinch themselves to the girth of your time,
then spend the day gathering grime anew.

Near Gary, you pass a white Camry
with patches of gray primer where paint
has chipped away and notice
a bumper sticker stuck to the trunk:
     "DRIVE NOW, TEXT LATER"
as it drifts into your lane, the driver
talking on his smart phone and eating
an egg McMuffin. It's the only time
you remember being thankful for toll booths.

Wisconsin is golden rust and mud,
its growth season bogging down in
the afterbirth of baled harvest.

At a bar in Minneapolis,
a man in a golf shirt at a table
of golf shirts calls you over as
you walk toward the door, asks if you
know where to find any strip clubs.
You smile, wave a hand, shake your head
and exit, wondering if something about
the way you look convinced him
you would know.

Cheyenne

A train horn blows a loud lonely song
    and blows,
        and blows,
twenty-three verses of overnight overture.

After a night in Grand Rapids filled
with raucous bikers racing the streets,
exhaust pipes piercing the tranquility,
Bertha insists on choosing our next stop:
an Econo Lodge outside Cheyenne.

You only want a place to park,
unwind, at the windblown end of a day
of touristing at Rushmore and Crazy Horse,
a place to find that fleeting rumor
of rest vacations always promise.

Who knew the thick, alluring tree line
across the four-lane highway hid
six active sets of railroad tracks
or the hotel's upper floor was
set aside for *seasonal guests*?

When morning slinks down the hazy
side of a broken night. You decide
to skip the continental breakfast,
break for the hills on the far side
of the tracks. A pit bull chained

to the third floor hand rail objects
to the sound of suitcase rollers.
Someone yells, "*¡Cállate, perro!*"
as a shoe bounces off the dog's ass
and lands on the hood of a van below.

Perro no habla español.
After a yelp and a whimper,
he resumes a dogged serenade.
A train howls a reply, and you don't
wait around for the other shoe to fall.

Math Don't Lie

You should have gassed up in Louisville,
before you crossed the Ohio, before
the blank stare of southern Illinois
forced you to consider distance

versus tank reserve. You know math
always wins these matchups and math
now says you should have stopped
in Louisville, but traffic was polite

as rush hour loomed. You could steer
clear of the gnarly wake commuters make
on their way home. You were certain
a cluster of fuel and fast food options

huddled on the far side of the river.
You passed them your last trip through.
Or was that a different road? After
a while, some stretches look so much alike.

Southern Ohio, southern Indiana,
southern Illinois, each has its own
Mt. Vernon with mileage signs to match.
Here the road sign said one hundred

and sixty-seven miles. Your reserve
said one hundred and seventy, close
but there had to be at least one station
on this section of interstate, surely

a savvy entrepreneur reasoned
a pit stop between Louisville
and Mt. Vernon was a certain
moneymaker. *If you build it,*

they will come. So you twist open
the throttle in southern Illinois
where wide treeless plains leave nowhere
for stealthy cops to hide. It's just you

and the long haulers you fly by
at ninety-five miles an hour. You,
fresh air, sunshine, open road:
What could possibly go wrong?

After an hour of full throttle,
a road sign says sixty-nine miles
to Mt. Vernon, but your fuel gauge
now says fifty-eight. Math has turned

against you. You saw the map before
you left: nothing between Louisville
and Mt. Vernon and now you
can testify to its accuracy.

Math says: speed kills fuel consumption,
so you slow to seventy, scour
every green sign, every billboard
for hope, but there's nothing and your gauge

continues its constant rate of drain:
fifty-one miles of road, forty-six miles
of gas. You slow again. Truckers you passed
an hour earlier now pass you back.

You swear you hear a snicker in
the tone of their exhaust, a laughing
confirmation that they've been this way
before and always refuel in Louisville.

You wonder how long it would take
triple A to reach you if your tank runs dry.
Could your cell phone get a signal here?
Would they have to come from Louisville?

Twenty-nine miles of road left, twenty-three
miles of gas. You imagine yourself coasting
down an exit ramp outside Mt. Vernon,
rolling in neutral until inertia deserts you.

A *Flying J* down the road raspberries you,
taunts you with a mantra you've heard
in your head for the last sixty-nine miles:
You should have stopped in Louisville.

Pacing Yourself

You're doing seventy in a fifty-five
in heavy fog on a winding highway
in Tennessee, a white Ram pickup
snuggles so close behind you can count
dead bugs on its chrome grill.

You're doing seventy in a fifty-five
snaking up the western slopes
of the Appalachians, through fog
so thick it runs like rain blown
sideways across your windshield.

You're doing seventy-five in a fifty-five,
a chain of semis crawls up the right lane,
a white Ram pickup chases you uphill—
no doubt a local who's late for work, late
for breakfast, late for brain surgery.

You're doing eighty in a fifty-five,
a slick climb, a local yokel humping
your rear fender, two dots ahead
flash red, signal imminent danger,
a clustered rendezvous, ending badly.

The mountain finally finds its top,
a weigh station sucks the trucks aside, clears
the right lane. You slide over, slow, watch
an uncorked crush of commuters burst
into open space and spar for the lead.

You're doing sixty-five down the bright side
of a murky mountain lost in mirrors smeared
with dew. Gloved hands grip damp handlebars,
a sweat-sheened destiny rushes you downhill,
skittering out of each electric curve.

You Know These Roads

Sometimes you think you could travel
these roads blindfolded, close your eyes
and find your way home or somewhere
familiar, a street name you know,
a billboard that hasn't changed
in decades, a diner parked
conveniently close to the road
with a neon sign that says *Open*.

Exit signs you pass post the names
of towns, roads, route numbers etched
into your memory in *Day-Glo* paint,
a distance in miles you translate
into seasons, events, years gone by;
people populating pages
in an unscripted journal
of an unplotted journey
toward an unknown destination
with mile markers as captions to hint
at what came before or waits ahead.

Each road sign implies one thing,
your rearview mirror another:

    Town where you were born
    Town where you grew up
    Town that closes at 5pm and all day on Sundays
    Town found when lost on an ill-advised shortcut
    Town with no gas station
    Ghost town

Town where Matilda, your '65
        Ambassador, cracked her block
        and was put to rest
Town where you left your wallet and didn't
        discover it missing until the next time
        you stopped for gas 200 miles away
Town where your grandmother was born
Town where you experienced your first
        passionate kiss and second orgasm
        (maybe third)
Town where you left your first love
        forever
Town where your best friend was married
Bean Town
Town where your roommate's father died
        of a heart attack
Town where his son died from overdose
Town where your son was born
        and his son
Town with a pond and clock tower
        in the main square and boarded up
        buildings all around.
Town where the fan belt broke on the old
        Chevelle along with the water pump
        at 10pm on a Saturday night
Town of rocking chairs
Town with bears in bonnets and sunglasses
Town with three colleges
        three golf courses

three micro-brews
three sisters
and bike lanes
Moose town
Town where a pair of flats meant sleeping
      in the bed of your truck in the rain
Town where you pissed in the underground walkway
      because it smelled like everyone else had
Town where you slept with spiders
      under cardboard, behind junipers,
      against a brick wall
Town where you ran dry on the exit ramp
      two miles short of a Chevron station,
      in the middle of a State Trooper
      dragnet for escaped prisoners
Town where an old black man excused himself
      when you walked past him where he sat
Town where a store clerk refused you service
      when you asked another patron, a hunter,
      a black man, what his favorite game was
Town of marchers with picket signs,
      of broken windshields and tires shredded
      by sharpened jacks
Steel town
Town where you got a ticket for parking
      in an unmarked handicap zone
City where your mother was arrested
      as a teenage runaway and locked up
      with prostitutes

Town where you ran away and camped
    on a hill for two weeks in mid-winter
Town where you hitched a ride with a guy in a Nova
    you were convinced (later) was a serial killer
Town where you were exiled after burning
    too many bridges at your previous stop
Town where you were caught on the wrong side
    of the Rockies in a late May snow storm
Windy city
Town of broad shoulders, box cars,
    double trailers, and toll roads
Town where two guys tried to rob you,
    then bought you a beer when they learned
    you were more broke than they were
Town where Barney Fife pulled you
    and a cute blonde over for speeding,
    but only tagged you
Town where Johnny Carson was born
Town that barely made the map and smelled
    like cow shit because it had fifty times
    as many cattle as people
Town you cut through at 2am
    on a Halloween bender to find
    a haunted house and were escorted out
    by local cops
Town where you jumped a moving train
Town where you broke your foot in three places
    jumping off a moving train
Town with the same name as twenty
    other towns in twenty other states

Town where you learned how not to ride
    a bicycle when your friend was skewered
    through the neck by handlebars
Town where you witnessed your first violent death,
    a bicyclist hit by a drunk driver,
    his body wedged into a split against the curb
    with one leg twisted behind his head
Town where a Pomeranian defended
    its owner's shrubs from a bull elk grazing
Dream town
City of bright lights, beautiful people
    and highways
Town where you wish you could live
Town where you hope to die.

Where You Are

You are here
            and here
            and here.
Every rest stop tries
to red-arrow you into place
on a piece of paper framed
behind glass to protect it
from bleary-eyed graffiti
and wayward steerage.

You were there
            and there.
You remember going off-
road to stretch your legs, test
the local cuisine. Your waitress
migrated from Austin, bright
eyes, pretty smile, she forgot
you soon after your tip met
the bottom of her apron.

You are here
            going there.
Your map is a jumble of rusty
road signs, scarred vehicles,
blurred landscapes, faces
in silhouette. You're a ghost
passing through the walls of lives
with no fixed destination,
but a tireless need to say
you've been somewhere.

Special Thanks

As writers, we often find ourselves banging around inside our own heads. When we finally poke out and bring with us words we believe to be literary art; words we want others to consider art, it's nice to have friends and colleagues help us finesse the raw materials of our solitude into something we can present to the rest of the world. I'd like to thank members of my extended writer family for their feedback and thoughtfulness, but before I do, I must thank my lovely wife, Jill Rausch, whose patience and support are legendary. Seriously. There are plaques hanging as evidence in at least 2 states and poems written in her honor.

Among those who helped shape this book: Jonathan K. Rice, Anne Kaylor, Richard Peabody, Maria Rouphail, Alice Osborne, Shawn Pavey, Cathy Smith Bowers, Steve Taylor, Richard Allen Taylor, Eric Weil, Dave Essinger, Leslie Anne McIlroy, John Yewell and Mimi Herman, the second floor crew at the Quality Inn Lafayette, Kathie Giorgio for inviting me to the AllWriter's Retreat in Northfield, Il where much of this book was roughed out as well as the other retreat attendees whose feedback convinced me I had material worth pursuing. Among them Gwen Ackerman, Lynne Carol Austin, Sue Bartenstein, Julie Beekman, Linda Benjamin, Alice Benson, Byron Brumbaugh, Barb Geiger, Michael Giorgio, Colleen Glatzel, Anita Golden-Burrell, Jen Hocevar, Marcia Marino, Colleen McKinney, Carrie Newberry, Lila Schwenk, Johannah Siragusa, Theresa Smith, and Christopher Werkman.

MSD

M. Scott Douglass is publisher, managing editor, and book designer at Main Street Rag Publishing Company which he helped found in 1996. He grew up in Pittsburgh, attended Penn State-Behrend (Erie, PA) and has a graphic arts degree from Central Piedmont Community College in Charlotte. Aside from those mentioned in the acknowledgments, his poetry has appeared in such places as *Redheadded Stepchild, The Southeast Review (Sundog), Southern Poetry Review,* and *Wild Goose Review* (among others). He's been a Pushcart Prize nominee and the recipient of a 2001 NC Arts & Science Council Emerging Artist Grant which was used to publish his first full-length poetry collection, *Auditioning for Heaven* (an honorable mention for the 2001 Brockman Campbell Award). In 2010, the Poetry Council of North Carolina dedicated its annual, *Bay Leaves,* to M. Scott Douglass for his support of poets and poetry in the state of North Carolina. His cover designs have garnered two PICA Awards and a 2010 Eric Hoffer Award nomination for graphic design.

Off the field (so to speak), he's been a dental technician, a construction/demolition worker, a bookstore owner, baseball and basketball coach. He bred rats for the University of Pittsburgh's Pathology Department and even wrestled a lion once. Yes, a real lion.